WORLD ALMANAC® LIBRARY
OF THE
AMERICAN REVOLUTION

The American Colonies Declare Independence

Dale Anderson

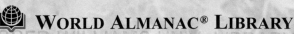
WORLD ALMANAC® LIBRARY

Please visit our web site at: www.worldalmanaclibrary.com

For a free color catalog describing World Almanac® Library's list of high-quality books and multimedia programs, call 1-800-848-2928 (USA) or 1-800-387-3178 (Canada). World Almanac® Library's fax: (414) 332-3567.

Library of Congress Cataloging-in-Publication Data

Anderson, Dale, 1953-
    The American colonies declare independence / by Dale Anderson.
       p. cm. — (World Almanac Library of the American Revolution)
    Includes bibliographical references and index.
    ISBN 0-8368-5926-X (lib. bdg.)
    ISBN 0-8368-5935-9 (softcover)
    1. United States—History—Revolution, 1775-1783—Juvenile literature. 2. United States—History—Revolution, 1775-1783—Campaigns—Juvenile literature. 3. United States—Politics and government—1775-1783—Juvenile literature. I. Title. II. Series.
    E208.A52   2005
    973.3—dc22   2005040813

First published in 2006 by
World Almanac® Library
A Member of the WRC Media Family of Companies
330 West Olive Street, Suite 100
Milwaukee, WI 53212 USA

Produced by Discovery Books
Editor: Sabrina Crewe
Designer and page production: Sabine Beaupré
Photo researcher: Sabrina Crewe
Maps and diagrams: Stefan Chabluk
Consultant: Andrew Frank, Assistant Professor of History, Florida Atlantic University
World Almanac® Library editorial direction: Mark J. Sachner
World Almanac® Library editor: Alan Wachtel
World Almanac® Library art direction: Tammy West
World Almanac® Library production: Jessica Morris

Photo credits: Brown University Library: pp. 27, 35; CORBIS: pp. 11, 19, 33, 37; Independence National Historical Park: title page, pp. 22, 25, 34; Library of Congress: pp. 28, 39, 42; National Archives: pp. 38, 40; National Park Service: pp. 8, 12; North Wind Picture Archives: cover, pp. 5, 7, 13, 15, 16, 21, 29, 31.

Printed in Canada

1 2 3 4 5 6 7 8 9 09 08 07 06 05

Front cover: In July 1776, thirteen British colonies in North America declared their independence from Britain. This print shows a joyous crowd gathered outside Independence Hall in Philadelphia to hear the Declaration of Independence.

Title page: James Peale painted this portrait of George Washington on horseback in about 1790. He based the portrait on a work by his brother, Charles Willson Peale—the faces of both the brothers can be seen on the left, behind Washington. In the background on the right are Revolutionary soldiers, one carrying a French flag.

Contents

In 1776, the thirteen British **colonies** along the eastern coast of North America declared themselves independent of Britain. The colonists were already fighting British soldiers in protest at British policies. In 1781, the British surrendered to American forces, and, in 1783, they formally recognized the colonies' independence.

A New Nation

The movement from colonies to independence, known as the American Revolution, gave birth to a new nation—the United States of America. Eventually, the nation stretched to the Pacific Ocean and grew to comprise fifty states. Over time, it was transformed from a nation of farmers into an industrial and technological giant, the world's richest and most powerful country.

An Inspiration to Others

The American Revolution was based on a revolution of ideas. The people who led the American Revolution believed that the purpose of government was to serve the people, not the reverse. They rejected rule by monarchs and created in its place a **republic**. The founders of the republic later wrote a **constitution** that set up this form of government and guaranteed people's basic rights, including the right to speak their minds and the freedom to worship as they wished.

The ideals on which the United States of America was founded have inspired people all around the world ever since. Within a few years of the American Revolution, the people of France had risen up against their monarchy. Over time, the people of colonies in Central

British colonists in North America had no elected representatives in Parliament, shown here in the 1700s. This fact caused deep resentment in the colonies, especially when Parliament imposed taxes and harsh laws.

and South America, in Asia, and in Africa followed the U.S. example and rebelled against their position as colonists. Many former colonies have become independent nations.

Tension in the Colonies

In 1774, however, all that lay in the future. Americans were still British colonists, but there was a feeling of rising anger in the colonies. For the previous ten years, Britain's government—called Parliament— had imposed a series of taxes on the colonies. Colonists known as **Patriots** had protested. The protests angered British leaders, who thought of the Patriots as rebels.

In December 1773, Patriots in Boston, Massachusetts, had dumped cases of tea belonging to a British company into Boston Harbor in a dramatic protest. The British had promptly closed the port, placed troops in the city, and shut down the elected governments of the city and of the colony of Massachusetts.

In the fall of 1774, colonial leaders met in Philadelphia at the First Continental **Congress**. They asked Britain's King George III to end the harsh policies. They also urged colonists to stop buying British goods and to form **militia** units. The Congress decided to meet again in the spring of 1775 to judge the British response. Meanwhile, colonists turned their eyes to Boston, where a few thousand British troops sat inside the city, surrounded by angry Patriots.

CHAPTER ONE

The Battle of Lexington and Concord

British general Thomas Gage—governor of Massachusetts and commander of British military forces in North America—was well aware of the colonists' anger. He became especially worried when he learned that Patriots from several towns were taking their supplies of gunpowder out of the colony's main **arsenal** at Somerville.

An Uneasy Peace

On September 1, 1774, Gage sent soldiers to seize the gunpowder remaining in the arsenal, about 250 half-barrels. The seizure inflamed the Patriots, and a few thousand men from Massachusetts and Connecticut assembled in Cambridge, across the river from Boston. Gage closed Boston off from the countryside by stationing troops across the thin neck of land that was the only entrance into the city.

The situation remained tense. With the colonial **legislature** shut down, Patriots in Massachusetts formed a temporary government they called the Provincial Congress. They chose a dashing Patriot doctor, Joseph Warren, as president. Militia companies began to train frequently on the village greens, the common areas in the center of each Massachusetts town.

Militia and Minutemen

In the British colonies, all males aged sixteen to fifty joined militia units and trained to fight so they would be ready to protect their communities and colonies if necessary. Massachusetts had a tradition of militia service dating back to the founding of the colony in the 1600s. In 1774, the Massachusetts Provincial Congress suggested that towns take one-third of their men to form "minute companies" made up of men who would be ready to fight at a minute's notice. This, too, was based on tradition dating from the 1600s. Several towns did form minuteman units, but not all of them. Both militiamen and minutemen came from all walks of life— they included farmers, teachers, and doctors.

Militiamen leave home to fight the British during the American Revolution.

Problems for General Gage

Gage was well informed of these developments because **Loyalists** regularly helped the British by reporting on the militias' activities. British army scouts also rode across the countryside, learning more about local communities and attitudes. The more Gage learned, the more he worried. He had only about three thousand soldiers, while the Patriots could muster many times that number.

When Gage wrote to Britain asking for reinforcements, British officials sent only a few hundred Royal Marines.

In February 1775, Gage sent some troops north to Salem to seize Patriot cannons. The troops ran into a large force of Salem militia, which refused to let them pass. More militia arrived from nearby towns. Outnumbered, the British force withdrew, mocked by the colonists as they marched back.

Orders from Britain

In the following weeks, there were several clashes between colonists and soldiers in Massachusetts that nearly erupted into full-fledged fights. In April 1775, Gage received new orders from Britain. The stalemate had to end, he was told. He had to take action against the rebels—and soon.

Preparations

Gage decided to march northwest to Concord to seize weapons stored there by the Patriots. Gage knew that Samuel Adams and John Hancock,

First Step

"It is the opinion of the King's servants, in which His Majesty concurs, that the first and essential step to be taken towards re-establishing government, would be to arrest and imprison the principal actors . . . of the Provincial Congress."

British government's orders to General Thomas Gage, 1775

two leading Patriots, were staying in Lexington, a town on the road to Concord. In spite of British orders, however, he never ordered their arrest.

The British spent the next two weeks preparing the expedition in utmost secrecy. The road west out of Boston and then north to Concord passed many hills, which could be used by the militia to ambush the troops. So Gage planned for his army to cross the Charles River by boat and then march west to Concord. He put Lieutenant Colonel Francis Smith in charge. Second in command was Major John Pitcairn, a fiery marine. The two would command a force of about eight hundred soldiers.

The steeple of Old North Church in Boston, shown here, was used to display a signal about British troop movements. On the night of April 18, 1775, the light from two lanterns let Patriots know that the soldiers were on their way.

Gage also sent out mounted troops to patrol the roads north and west of Boston and arrest any colonists sent to warn Concord of the soldiers' approach. Patriot spies in Boston, however, had already learned of the plans and warned their allies in Concord, who had moved most of the weapons out of town.

Alerting the Patriots

Meanwhile, Dr. Warren kept a close eye on British troop movements. His fellow Patriot Paul Revere set up a system for alerting the countryside when the British finally marched. Patriot William Dawes would ride out of Boston Neck and then turn north. Revere himself would head north from Charlestown to Medford and spread the alarm along the way.

On the night of April 18, 1775, the British troops finally moved. So did Dawes and Revere. After crossing from Boston to Charlestown, Revere mounted a horse and raced west. As he reached each town, he shouted, "The **regulars** are out!" In other words, British troops were on the way. Patriots in each town called

This map shows Boston and the nearby towns where the American Revolution began. It also shows the movements of British troops and Patriot militia who took part in the Battle of Lexington and Concord.

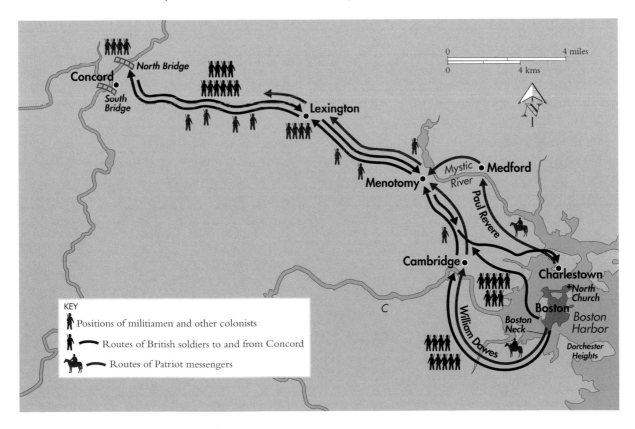

KEY

Positions of militiamen and other colonists

Routes of British soldiers to and from Concord

Routes of Patriot messengers

What Happened to the Messengers?

On the way to Concord, Revere and Dawes met Doctor Samuel Prescott, returning home to Concord after visiting his fiancée in Lexington. Prescott agreed to help spread the alarm. Soon after, the three riders were met by a British patrol. Prescott slipped away and reached Concord with the news of the British march. Dawes escaped in another direction and returned to Lexington. Revere was captured and returned to Lexington, but released before the fighting began.

out the militia, and some sent their own riders out to spread the news to yet other towns. Revere, meanwhile, continued to Lexington.

At about midnight, Revere reached the house where Hancock and Adams were staying. (Dawes arrived some time later.) He warned the leaders to flee for safety. After resting briefly, Revere and Dawes raced off toward Concord.

On Lexington Green

In Lexington, militia commander Captain John Parker sent out two scouts. The first returned soon after with nothing to report, but near dawn the second scout finally reappeared. The British were on their way, he reported, and very near.

In the early morning hours of April 19, Parker and about 70 militia men gathered on the town green. Soon, Major Pitcairn and the British advance guard—about 250 men—appeared. "Throw down your arms, you villains, you rebels!" yelled Pitcairn. By some reports, Parker ordered his men to disperse and let the British pass.

The First Shot

Then someone—no one knows who—fired a shot. Ignoring the shouted orders of their officers, British troops followed with a volley that left several militiamen dead and a number of

Ill-Planned Expedition

"This expedition . . . from beginning to end was as ill-planned and ill-executed as it was possible to be."

Lieutenant John Barker, part of Lt. Col. Smith's force at Lexington and Concord, 1775

The first battle of the American Revolution, on Lexington Green, took the lives of several Patriots. It still isn't known which side fired the first shot that led to the battle.

others wounded. Next, the British charged with fixed **bayonets** at the militiamen and even at onlookers. Just then, Lt. Col. Smith and the main body of troops arrived. Angered by the chaos, Smith got his officers to restore order, but not before eight colonists had been killed.

Reaching Concord

Many officers thought they should turn back, but Smith ordered the force to march on. They reached Concord a few hours later. The militia from Concord and nearby Lincoln saw they were badly outnumbered by the British. They withdrew and left the town to the soldiers.

Smith's troops began looking for weapons but found only three cannons and a few lead musket balls. The British began burning the carriages of the guns, and the fire spread to a nearby building. The militiamen who had gathered west of the town saw the fire and grew angry because they thought the British were burning Concord. They advanced toward the small British force guarding a bridge over the Concord River. One of the British soldiers—disobeying orders—fired, and soon the two forces were shooting at each other. The British retreated to Concord in a panic.

Easy Targets

By the time the British came back toward North Bridge with reinforcements, the colonists had taken up positions behind stone walls. The British, out in the open, made easy targets. Thinking that his soldiers had found all the supplies they would find

This bridge that crosses Concord River today is a replica of North Bridge, where fighting took place in 1775.

Rebel Spirit

"The Rebels are not the despicable rabble too many have supposed them to be, and I find it owing to a military spirit encouraged amongst them for a few years past, joined with an uncommon degree of zeal and enthusiasm."

Thomas Gage, letter to the Earl of Dartmouth in Britain, 1775

in Concord, and sensing growing danger, Smith decided to turn back.

At about noon, Smith's force began a long and bloody march back to Boston. The British had more than 17 miles (27 kilometers) to go to reach safety. Colonial militia plagued the British during the entire retreat. Between Concord and Lexington,

hundreds of militia gathered at bends in the road and other favorable sites. When the British appeared, they would fire, killing and wounding several with each attack. The Lexington militia grouped at one spot, itching for revenge. They had the satisfaction of wounding Colonel Smith himself.

A Relief Division Arrives

At Lexington, however, the British troops found a welcome sight. Gage had sent a relief division of several hundred soldiers with two cannons. They reached Lexington from the east just before Smith's retreating troops arrived from the west. The men had arrived just in time—Smith's troops were tired, wounded, and confused.

The British regrouped their forces and pulled out of Lexington shortly after three o'clock. It took the British

The British soldiers were exposed to fire on all sides as they made their way back from Concord toward Boston. Militiamen shot at them from houses and behind fences, rocks, and trees.

four or five more hours to reach Charlestown, and the fierce fighting continued all the way back. Between seven and eight, the surviving British troops collapsed on the banks of the Charles River.

Incessant Fire

"We [retreated] under an incessant fire, which like a moving circle surrounded and followed us wherever we went."

Hugh Percy, commander of the British relief force sent to Lexington, 1775

CHAPTER TWO

Preparing for War

Warfare between the British and the Patriots at Lexington and Concord signaled the beginning of the American Revolutionary war. There was no turning back.

The British expedition to Concord had been a disaster. In return for burning three cannons, the British suffered significant numbers of **casualties**. About 70 soldiers were killed, and approximately another 200 were wounded or missing. The colonists suffered 50 deaths, and about 40 people were reported wounded.

Reports of the Battle

The Patriots soon spread word of the conflict— within a week, the message had traveled from Maine to Philadelphia. Within another two weeks, word reached the southern colonies. Anger against the British—and fear—spread through the colonies. In Virginia, lawyer Thomas Jefferson wrote that a "frenzy of revenge seems to have seized all ranks of people."

Dr. Warren gathered eyewitness accounts from Massachusetts people about British actions, such as stories of British soldiers entering homes,

Barbarous Murders

"The barbarous murders of our innocent brethren . . . has made it absolutely necessary that we immediately raise an army to defend our wives and our children from the butchering hands of an inhuman soldiery."

Joseph Warren, appealing to other colonies for soldiers, 1775

taking property, burning houses, or threatening women. Massachusetts newspapers published stories that blamed the British for all the fighting.

Support for Massachusetts

The Provincial Congress called on other colonies to send troops to the Boston area. The colonists' force swelled to about 15,000 men, with Artemas Ward of Massachusetts in command. Ward sent about half the force to Roxbury, south of Boston, to ensure that the British could not move onto the mainland over Boston Neck. The rest Ward kept in camps in Cambridge, as he tried to figure out what to do next.

British soldiers enter the home of a colonial family to take their property. Incidents such as this were reported around the colonies and in Britain, gaining sympathy for the Patriot cause.

The News Arrives in Britain

In late April 1775, Warren learned that Gage was sending an official report of Lexington and Concord to Britain. Warren put together eye-witness accounts, added an open letter to the British people, and hired a ship to carry the documents to Britain. The documents, portraying the army as villains and the colonists as victims, reached London two weeks before Gage's report. They had the desired effect. One British politician noted gloomily, "The Bostonians are now the favorites of all the people of good hearts and weak heads in the kingdom."

Ethan Allen (holding a sword), leader of Vermont's Green Mountain Boys, confronts the British commander of Fort Ticonderoga on May 10, 1775, and demands that the British surrender.

Meanwhile, Gage did little to organize his army or confront the growing colonial militia. Morale among the British forces plunged.

Fort Ticonderoga

In May 1775, the Massachusetts militia tried an offensive far to the west of Boston. Benedict Arnold, an officer from Connecticut, suggested seizing Fort Ticonderoga on New York's Lake Champlain and capturing its cannons.

When he got to Fort Ticonderoga, Arnold found that Ethan Allen, leader of a militia unit called the Green Mountain Boys, had the same idea. Allen and Arnold joined forces in an attack on May 10. The British **garrison**—and the fort's cannons—fell easily into the Americans' hands.

Ethan Allen (1738–1789)

Born in Connecticut, Ethan Allen moved to what is now the state of Vermont and became colonel of the Green Mountain Boys. Until the Revolution, the Green Mountain Boys' major activity was to harass settlers who had land grants in the Vermont region, which was then claimed by both New York and New Hampshire. After capturing Fort Ticonderoga, Allen led a failed attempt to take Montreal, Canada, in September 1775. He spent the next few years as a British prisoner. Once he was released, Allen returned to Vermont, where he again attacked settlers. He pleaded unsuccessfully with the Congress to make Vermont an independent state. Only two years after Allen's death, however, Vermont gained statehood.

The Second Congress

Also on May 10, **delegates** gathered in Philadelphia for the Second Continental Congress. They came from all the colonies except Georgia. The delegates from Massachusetts included John Hancock, Samuel Adams, and Adams's cousin John Adams, a lawyer committed to the idea of American independence. Virginia's group included George Washington, Richard Henry Lee, and Thomas Jefferson. Pennsylvania sent the experienced Benjamin Franklin and the highly respected John Dickinson.

The Congress Acts

The Congress heard reports of the fighting outside Boston and received Dr. Warren's request that it set up an army. On June 14, 1775, the Congress approved a plan to raise troops in some of the colonies and send them to Boston. It also made plans for a new national army, the American Continental Army, and agreed to borrow money to finance the army.

The Congress chose several generals to lead its forces. For commander in chief of the Patriot military and leader of the Continental army, the Congress selected George Washington. Washington had gained military experience in the French and Indian War and had trained some militia troops, but he was also chosen for political reasons. The delegates hoped to gain more support in the South by naming a southerner and slave owner.

CHAPTER THREE

Battling around Boston

News of Lexington and Concord had alarmed the British government. Officials worried that General Gage was not the right man for the situation. They dispatched more troops and three major generals —William Howe, Henry Clinton, and John Burgoyne—to Boston to assist Gage.

The Situation in Boston

When they arrived on May 25, 1775, the generals were shocked by the low morale of the British troops. They were also distressed by the army's dangerous position in Boston, hemmed in by large numbers of Patriots. Even worse, in their opinion, General Gage had made no effort to capture the high ground north of the city, near Charlestown, or to the south, the Dorchester Heights. If the Patriots grabbed those hills and planted cannons on them, the British would be in grave danger.

Too Much for Gage

"I must lament that General Gage, with all his good qualities, finds himself in a situation of too great importance for his talents. . . . I doubt whether Mr. Gage will venture to take a single step beyond his instructions, or whether the troops have that opinion of him as to march with confidence of success."

George, Lord Germain, British secretary of state for the colonies, 1775

The Patriots Build Defenses

Gage made plans to seize the hills, but once again the Patriot spy network was at work. The militia decided to seize the hills near Charlestown before the British could. On 16 June, after dark, Patriot leader Artemas Ward sent Israel Putnam of Connecticut and William Prescott of Massachusetts with about one thousand men. The militia started digging a **redoubt** on Breed's Hill, and by dawn on June 17, they had walls that were about 6 feet (2 meters) high.

The British Respond

On seeing the Patriot militia at work, the British commanders agreed that they had to attack before the Patriots became too entrenched. Howe was given command of the operation, which included over two thousand British soldiers. The first troops landed on the Charlestown

A Misnamed Battle

The battle fought in June 1775 has gone down in history as the Battle of Bunker Hill, a misleading name. The fighting actually took place on nearby Breed's Hill, where the colonists built their main defenses. A monument to the battle stands today on the actual battle-ground, Breed's Hill. Bowing to popular custom, however, it is called the Bunker Hill Monument.

peninsula just past noon on June 17. But the attack could not yet begin; the boats that brought those troops needed to return to Boston to bring more soldiers.

The delay helped the Patriots. They realized that the British planned to attack a thin line of troops that stretched north from the redoubt. So they moved more militia to the area, stationing some behind a rail fence north of the redoubt and others on a beach along Mystic River.

The Patriots had to work under a steady stream of cannon fire from the

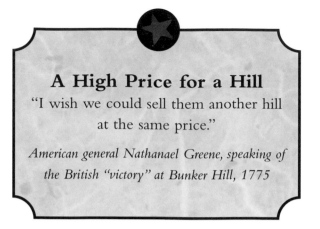

A High Price for a Hill

"I wish we could sell them another hill at the same price."

American general Nathanael Greene, speaking of the British "victory" at Bunker Hill, 1775

British ships and from **batteries** in Boston. Some shells struck the town of Charlestown, which soon became a raging mass of flame.

The Battle of Bunker Hill

Howe planned three troop movements against the American defenses. General Sir Robert Pigot was to lead one body of troops against the

This map shows the Charlestown peninsula, where the Battle of Bunker Hill took place in June 1775. The main fighting actually took place on Breed's Hill, where Patriot militia had built defenses.

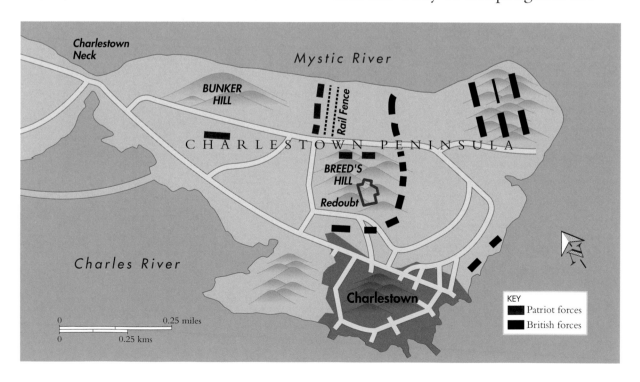

KEY
Patriot forces
British forces

The British lost many troops as they advanced in the Battle of Bunker Hill because the Americans held several strong positions from which to fire on the soldiers. The British eventually regained control of the Charlestown peninsula.

redoubt. Meanwhile, Howe would lead the main body of his army against the men behind the rail fence. A third group would move along the Mystic River shore north of that fence and swing around to attack the Patriots from behind. After they had overrun the rail fence, the other

British forces would join Pigot's in taking the redoubt.

Three things spoiled Howe's plan. First, the British had, unbelievably, brought the wrong size of ammunition for the field cannon that was supposed to blow holes in the Patriot lines. The cannons, therefore, were

Joseph Warren (1741–1775)

After graduating from Harvard College at age eighteen, Joseph Warren became a physician. The Stamp Act crisis of 1765 brought him into politics, where he became friends with Samuel Adams, John Hancock, and other Patriots. Warren was highly regarded for his organizing ability and his writing. An early leader of the Patriots in Boston, Warren was killed at Bunker Hill. The Patriots deeply mourned his death. Months after Warren died, his friend Paul Revere recovered Warren's body, which was identified by the false teeth Revere himself had made for the doctor.

useless. Second, the militia troops on the beach blocked the advance with deadly rifle fire. Within minutes, the British withdrew from that area with nearly a hundred soldiers dead on the beach. Third, the Patriot militia troops at the rail fence unexpectedly held their ground and returned fire when the British soldiers were at close range. The British troops fell back, leaving many dead and wounded on the field.

The Final Assault

Howe rallied his forces for a second attack, but it had the same result as the first. At four in the afternoon, Howe was ready for a third assault, directing most of his force on the redoubt. By this time, however, Howe had received a few hundred reinforcements, and the Patriots had just about run out of ammunition. As a result, the British were able to take the redoubt and send Patriot forces scrambling away. Joseph Warren—wearing a satin waistcoat trimmed with lace—fell to his death. So, too, did Britain's Major John Pitcairn, who had fought at Lexington and Concord.

Overwhelmed, the Patriot militia units pulled out of Breed's Hill. The forces on Bunker Hill fled west as well. By nightfall on June 17, the British held the Charlestown penin-sula. The cost of gaining that land, though, was huge. Out of a force of 2,500 or so, the British lost more than 200 men, and more than 800 were wounded. The Patriots had over 100 dead and about 300 wounded.

Washington Takes Charge

The British had beaten the militia off Charlestown's hills, but they were still trapped in Boston, surrounded by about 15,000 militiamen. On July 3, 1775, George Washington, who had arrived outside the city, officially took command of the American forces.

Wounded Troops

"After the battle, the king's wounded troops were carried to Boston; and it was truly a shocking sight and sound, to see the carts loaded with those unfortunate men, and to hear the piercing groans of the dying and of those [with] painful wounds."

Peter Oliver, Loyalist judge and observer of casualties at Bunker Hill, 1775

Washington was disheartened by what he saw. The troops were cocky and undisciplined. Worse, they were getting ready to go home—most of their terms of service would expire in several months' time.

Trapped in the City

The British were not in a much bet-ter position. Many troops had suffered greatly in the battle, and others con-tinued to grow frustrated from being cooped up in the city. While British officers enjoyed comfortable quar-ters—General Clinton, for instance, had taken over John Hancock's large house—their men were short of fresh food and would soon be plagued by a freezing winter. Meanwhile, it was clear that Gage was failing in his role as military commander. He was removed from command and replaced by William Howe.

CHAPTER FOUR

Debate among the Colonies

In early July 1775, the Second Continental Congress—still in session in Philadelphia—approved two **resolutions** that showed how the delegates were struggling to find the right response to British policy. Both documents were the work of Pennsylvania delegate John Dickinson.

Conflicting Resolutions

The first document, the Olive Branch Petition, was approved by the Congress on July 5. The petition was addressed to King George III, not to Parliament—the Patriots blamed Parliament for all the troubles and believed the king might intervene to help the colonists. After listing the colonists' complaints, the petition expressed hopes for peace and asked the king to stop further fighting until a reconciliation could be achieved.

The second document had a different tone. The "Declaration of the Causes and Necessities of Taking Up Arms" was approved on July 6. In stirring words, it declared the colonists' resolve to

Just Cause

"Our cause is just. Our union is perfect. Our internal resources are great, and, if necessary, foreign assistance is undoubtedly attainable. . . . We will, in defiance of every hazard . . . employ for the preservation of our liberties; being with one mind resolved to die freemen, rather than to live like slaves."

John Dickinson, "Declaration of the Causes and Necessities of Taking Up Arms," 1775

fight—and die if necessary—to resist British oppression. To reassure British "friends and fellow-subjects," however, the resolution promised not to bring an end to the bond between Britain and the colonies.

Three More Steps

Congress took three more steps that July. First, in mid-July, it appointed commissioners to negotiate peace treaties with Native American peoples and sent a message to the Iroquois of New York. The Congress feared that

A Family Quarrel

"This is a family quarrel between us and old England. You Indians are not concerned in it. We don't wish you to take up the hatchet against the King's troops. We desire you to remain at home, and not join on either side, but keep the hatchet buried deep. . . . What is it we have asked of you? Nothing but peace."

Continental Congress,
address to the Iroquois people, 1775

The Congress met in Philadelphia at the State House of the Province of Pennsylvania, now Independence Hall. The hall's assembly room, shown here, was the site of important decisions made by the Congress.

Indians might get involved in the conflict and threaten colonists who had settled on the western **frontier**.

Second, on July 26, the Congress established a post office department. It appointed Benjamin Franklin as postmaster general for the colonies.

The Congress's last action that month dismissed an earlier peace offer from Britain. Back in February 1775, British prime minister Frederick North had persuaded Parliament to approve a plan that recognized the Congress and dealt with the issue of taxation. The Congress rejected the plan because it did not address their concerns.

The Congress took a break between August 2 and September 12. The delegates then continued to meet throughout the war.

King George's Response

Meanwhile, on August 23, 1775, King George issued a proclamation that said the colonies were in open rebellion against Britain. In November, the Congress heard that the king had also rejected the Olive Branch Petition.

Although the king called it rebellion, the British government believed that the committed rebels were just a small minority of Americans. General Howe had written, "The insurgents are very few, in comparison with the whole of the people." The royal governors of North Carolina and Virginia made similar statements.

The British Plan

Based on these views, the king and government ministers agreed upon a plan. They would assemble a force of about twenty thousand men for an offensive the following spring. They would crush the Continental army and then, using the power of the Royal Navy, subdue the colonies.

Parliament eagerly backed the tough stance. In December 1775, it passed an act that banned any trade with the colonies. It went further, declaring that the navy could seize not only American ships and their cargoes, but those of any foreign country that traded with the colonists.

The Lines Harden

The king's dismissal of the Congress's petition did not sit well with colonists, nor did the use of words such as "traitor" or "rebel." The decision to hire **mercenaries** to fight in the colonies angered many Americans as well, as did Parliament's declaration of war on American shipping. Many formerly neutral colonists gave their support to the Patriots because of these actions.

The Congress responded to Parliament's actions with several tough steps. In October 1775, the delegates voted to form a navy. The next month, the Congress set up a secret committee charged with seeking foreign aid. In April 1776, it closed American ports to British ships.

Hiring Mercenaries

The British knew they needed a large army to fight the Americans. To fill the need for soldiers, the British turned to German princes, making contracts that paid the princes a sum for each soldier they supplied. The British promised that they would feed and equip the mercenaries during the course of the war. About 30,000 German mercenaries came to America to fight during the Revolution. The soldiers are often known as "Hessians" because many came from the region of Hesse–Cassel, but other areas of Germany supplied soldiers as well. Nearly 8,000 of the Germans died from wounds or disease; another 5,000 or so deserted. A few thousand Germans chose to make their homes in North America after the war.

Mercenary soldiers from Hesse-Cassel in Germany.

Temporary Leadership

The Continental Congress offered a strong and unifying leadership for the colonies during the Revolution, but it had no official standing. The structure of colonial government in the 1770s did not allow for any body that represented more than one colony. In addition, the delegates to the Congress had not been elected by the people of their colonies. Many colonial assemblies had been shut down by the British, and Patriot leaders simply formed new, unelected assemblies. It was these groups—formed in opposition to British law—that chose the delegates for the Continental Congress. While directing the course of the war, however, those delegates kept in mind the importance of establishing a representative government. Within days of the Declaration of Independence being approved in July 1776, John Dickinson presented to the Congress a suggested framework for government called the "Articles of Confederation and Perpetual Union."

An engraving of the Congress from the 1780s.

Adding to the outrage in the Congress and the colonies as a whole was a declaration from Virginia's royal governor, John, Lord Dunmore. In November 1775, he offered freedom to African American slaves who deserted their owners to fight in the British army. Resentment at Lord Dunmore's statement pushed many southern colonists, especially wealthy plantation owners, toward the Patriots' cause.

Lord Dunmore's Treachery

"Here you have a proclamation that will at once show the baseness of Lord Dunmore's heart, his malice and treachery against the people who were once under his government, and his officious violation of all law, justice, and humanity."

Anonymous letter to the Virginia Gazette *expresses Virginians' anger at their governor's support of the British, 1775*

A Divided Country

While the delegates at the Congress had reached agreement on several issues, the American colonists as a whole were divided about the future of their country. With war came more talk about independence, and there was a vocal minority of Patriots who now urged it. The percentage of these Patriots was higher in some areas—especially New England and Virginia—than in others, but they could be found in all the colonies.

While the Patriots had firm support, there was also a large segment of the population that remained attached to the British Crown. These people were known as Tories; now they are usually called Loyalists. Loyalists—like Patriots—could be found in all the colonies. Some areas had large numbers of Loyalists, including the middle colonies—New York, New Jersey, and Pennsylvania—plus South Carolina and Georgia in the South. But Loyalists were too scattered and often too different from each other in

Loyalists had their own newspapers during the Revolution, including the New-York Gazetteer, which circulated in Loyalist communities.

THURSDAY Nov. 23, 1775.   [Nº 136]

RIVINGTON's
NEW-YORK GAZETTEER;
OR,   THE
Connecticut, Hudson's River,   New-Jersey, and Quebec
WEEKLY ADVERTISER.
PRINTED at his OPEN and UNINFLUENCED PRESS fronting HANOVER-SQUARE.

Political Differences

"[Although] we may politically differ in sentiments, yet I see no reason, why privately we may not cherish the same esteem for each other, which formerly, I believe, subsisted between us. . . . We both of us seem to be steering opposite courses; the success of either lies in the womb of time. But whether it falls to my share or not, be assured that I wish you all health [and] happiness."

Loyalist John Randolph,
letter to Patriot Thomas Jefferson

ethnic origins or religion to become an effective political force. They did, however, form several fighting units to support the British army.

Persecution of Loyalists

About one-fifth of white people in the colonies were Loyalists. They suffered harassment by Patriot mobs and became victims of local laws. By the end of the Revolutionary War, many Loyalists had had their property taken by Patriot-run local governments and sold to the highest bidder.

In terms of Patriots and Loyalists, the American Revolution became a civil war. Both sides used violence,

William Franklin (1731–1813)

Son of Benjamin Franklin, William Franklin was a staunch Loyalist. Franklin served in the militia when young. From the 1750s, William Franklin worked closely with his father, traveling with him to Britain and acting as his assistant in both political and scientific work. In Britain, William Franklin secured the post of royal governor of New Jersey. He took the job in 1763. With a strong sense of duty and loyalty to the crown, William Franklin took the opposite side from his father before and during the Revolution and became a leader of the Loyalists. He returned to Britain in 1782, where he lived for the rest of his life. Ironically, William Franklin's own son—William Temple Franklin—rebelled against him and served as Benjamin Franklin's secretary during the latter's work as a **diplomat** in France.

Anti-Loyalist feeling ran high in the colonies during the American Revolution. This picture shows a group of Patriots exiling a Loyalist in a public and humiliating display.

and the conflict split many dear friends. In the end, thousands of Loyalists left what became the United States. Many moved to Britain, and some settled in British colonies in the West Indies. The great majority, however, moved north, where they became the founders of British Canada.

Banish the Loyalists

"Awake, Americans, to a sense of your danger. No time is to be lost—Instantly banish every Tory from among you. . . . Banishment, perpetual banishment, should be their lot."

Anonymous letter to the Pennsylvania Packet *newspaper, 1779*

CHAPTER FIVE

The Conflict Spreads

Attitudes to Canada, a British colony to the north, were mixed in the lower thirteen colonies. Canadians were mostly French Catholics, while the majority of the rebelling colonists were Protestants of British descent.

No Alliance with Canada

On the other hand, the Congress was willing to find allies wherever it could. So in late May 1775, the Congress sent an address to Canadians asking them to join the struggle against British tyranny. The Canadians declined the offer, prompting the Congress to launch an attack on Canada. The attack was a dismal failure.

In the South

Patriot forces enjoyed somewhat more success in the South when Americans gained control of the important port of Norfolk, Virginia, in December 1775. In January 1776, Governor Dunmore decided to shell the town in retaliation. He also sent groups to start fires. Winds spread the flames throughout the town, which burned for more than four days. Patriots reoccupied the town in February, but the burning of Norfolk increased Virginians' hatred of Dunmore.

In February 1776, Patriots also enjoyed a victory in North Carolina at Moore's Creek Bridge, near the town of Wilmington. In that victory, Patriots captured 850 men, about 1,500 guns, and loads of gold.

Back in Boston

While these events were taking place to the north and south, Washington and Howe still faced

General Richard Montgomery, center, was one of the leaders of the failed Patriot invasion of Canada in 1775. Although his forces captured Montreal, Montgomery was slain in the assault on Quebec.

The Invasion of Canada

The Congress approved a two-pronged invasion of Canada: one army would move up through New York to attack Montreal, while another would go through Maine to the St. Lawrence River to attack Quebec. An army under General Richard Montgomery occupied Montreal on November 13, 1775. Led by Benedict Arnold, the other Patriot force reached Quebec in November after a grueling journey, but was too exhausted to attack. In December, Montgomery—with about 300 men and some **artillery**—joined Arnold's force of around 650. The two generals decided they had to attack and launched an assault in a blizzard on the morning of December 31. Montgomery was killed immediately, and Arnold was just as quickly wounded. The attack failed miserably, with about 400 American soldiers taken prisoner. The Patriots maintained a weak **siege** outside the city until the spring of 1776, when the British forced them to retreat south.

Henry Knox was one of Washington's close advisors at the beginning of the American Revolution. Knox succeeded Washington as commander in chief of the military in 1783.

each other in Boston. The American general wanted to put more pressure on the British. He longed for the cannons taken from the British at Fort Ticonderoga back in May, but could not see how to get them overland. Colonel Henry Knox proposed a plan to get the cannons, which Washington accepted. In mid-November 1775, Knox left for New York.

Hardworking Rebels

"The rebels have done more work in one night than my whole army could do in months."

William Howe, on seeing the American defenses on Dorchester Heights, March 1776

Knox loaded the cannons onto sledges pulled by pairs of oxen and teams of men. The crews lugged nearly sixty artillery pieces—weighing about 60 tons—and ammunition through snow, over mountains, and down valleys. They reached Boston in late January 1776, a remarkable achievement.

Bringing the Guns to Bear

With the large guns now on hand, Washington sent American forces to take Dorchester Heights, the hills that rise to the south of Boston (see the map on page 9). The plan was to build two redoubts overnight. Then Knox's cannons could be placed inside and the positions used to shell Howe's troops and British ships in the harbor.

On the morning of March 5, 1776, the British awoke to find two Patriot strongholds where none had stood before. The British admirals warned Howe that once the redoubts had guns, their ships in Boston Harbor would be vulnerable. The ships would have to sail away, leaving Howe's force isolated. Howe developed a plan to attack Dorchester Heights, but it never took place. Perhaps remembering what happened on Breed's Hill, Howe decided to call off the attack before it began. A few days later, Howe announced it was time to leave Boston.

The British Depart

In mid–March 1776, the British prepared to leave the city. About 11,000 British troops marched down to the waiting ships. Joining them were about one thousand Loyalists, who were abandoning their homes.

Boston had suffered damage from the long occupation. During the cold winter of 1775–1776, many buildings had been taken down for firewood. Soldiers also did some looting on their way out of town.

American troops came happily into Boston after the British left. They found some usable cannons and a few thousand blankets.

Loyalists leave Boston

"[I] embarked for Halifax with [my] family consisting of a wife, six children and four servants, having only three days' notice to prepare [ourselves] for a voyage in a small ship crowded with near one hundred persons (exclusive of the ship's crew)."

Loyalist Richard Lechmere,
on the evacuation of Boston, 1776

The British ships eventually sailed to Halifax, Nova Scotia. Howe's army spent a miserable spring there while the general prepared his next move.

General Howe (center left, on horseback) supervises the evacuation of Boston. Thousands of soldiers are ferried out to ships while men (right) dump artillery in the harbor to keep it out of Patriot hands.

CHAPTER SIX

The Declaration

In January of 1776, meanwhile, opinion about the conflict with Britain was still divided. On January 9, a pamphlet appeared in Philadelphia that quickly became a sensation and influenced many people to support the idea of independence.

An Important Publication

Written anonymously by British writer Thomas Paine, the pamphlet entitled *Common Sense* proposed to offer the "simple facts, plain arguments, and common sense" of the Americans' situation. Paine said the problem was not Parliament, but the British monarchy. Kings, he stated, were always tyrants, and so it should be no surprise that George III was one, too.

Paine went on to say that Britain and America were two different places with two different peoples who had two different sets of interests. Remaining as colonies of Britain would only hurt America's trade and cost American lives. The only solution, he said, was independence. Americans needed no king—let them form their own government.

A Huge Circulation

Paine's pamphlet was a sensation. Within months, over 120,000 copies were sold, and eventually as many as 500,000 were in circulation. Those sales—huge in a country of 2.5 to 3 million people—do not reflect the pamphlet's actual reach, however. Copies were passed around, and many more people read Paine's words than actually bought the pamphlet.

Time to Part

"I challenge the warmest advocate for reconciliation, to show a single advantage that this continent can reap, by being connected with Great Britain. . . . Everything that is right or reasonable pleads for separation. The blood of the slain, the weeping voice of nature cries, 'tis time to part."

Thomas Paine, Common Sense, 1776

After the Revolution, Thomas Paine returned to Britain, but was outlawed for his writings and became a French citizen in 1792. Disgraced and jailed in France for political reasons, he came back to the United States, where he died penniless in New York in 1809.

Writing *Common Sense*

By the time he wrote *Common Sense,* Thomas Paine had been an unsuccessful corset maker, a fired tax collector, and a failed store keeper. He was introduced to Benjamin Franklin in Britain in 1774. Impressed by Paine's writing skill, Franklin dispatched Paine to America with letters of introduction. In Philadelphia, Paine met Dr. Benjamin Rush, a friend of Franklin's. Rush had been thinking of writing a pamphlet favoring independence but was concerned about the aftereffects. Many Philadelphians were Loyalists, and the doctor worried that he and his wife would be shunned and his medical practice would suffer. Would Paine be interested in writing it, he wondered? Paine was, and he took on the task with enthusiasm.

The Comee of the whole Congress to whom was referred the resolution and the Declaration respecting independence. — 17

Resolved That these united colonies are and of right ought to be free and independant states; that they are absolved from all allegiance to the british crown and that all political connection between them and the state of great Britain is and ought to be totally dissolved

Report & July 2. 1776
No 3 The resolution for indipendancy agreed to July 2. 1776

This is the original Lee Resolution— if the Congress approved the resolution, it would be declaring independence. The lines at the bottom right of the document indicated that twelve colonies voted to adopt the resolution on July 2, 1776.

Calls for Independence

Paine's pamphlet encouraged Americans to act. The first important step came from North Carolina. On April 12, 1776, the colony's Provincial Assembly agreed to instruct its delegates to the Continental Congress to vote in favor of independence. A month later, on May 15, Virginia's assembly told its delegates to go for independence. Meanwhile, on May 4, Rhode Island took a bigger step—it became the first colony to declare its own independence from Britain.

The Lee Resolution

On June 7, a member of the Congress presented an important resolution.

Virginia delegate Richard Henry Lee moved that, "These united colonies are and of right ought to be free and independent states; . . . and that all political connection between them and the State of Great Britain is and ought to be totally dissolved." John Adams seconded the Lee Resolution, but he knew that he had support from only nine of the thirteen colonies. The others had to be won over if the historic resolution was to proceed.

The Declaration of Independence

A meeting of the Declaration committee (from left): Thomas Jefferson, Roger Sherman, Benjamin Franklin, Robert Livingston, and John Adams.

In June 1776, while the colonies were still deciding about the Lee Resolution, a committee of five men was given the task of writing the Declaration of Independence. The actual writing fell to Thomas Jefferson, a brilliant thinker and a skilled writer. Jefferson turned out a masterpiece. The opening lines set forth the reason for the document itself: a "decent respect to the opinions of mankind" obliged the Congress to explain why it was declaring independence on behalf of the colonies. Jefferson outlined the natural rights that all people should have and the idea of the social contract—that is, that the government should serve the people who elect it. Jefferson then accused King George of "repeated injuries and usurpations" aimed at creating "an absolute tyranny over these states." Jefferson next described how the colonists patiently and repeatedly had asked the king to change his policies. Since their petitions had been ignored, the colonies would have to break with Britain and form a new nation. Members of the Congress, he said, were acting "by authority of the good people of these colonies."

Delegates began signing the official copy of the Declaration of Independence on August 2, 1776. The original document, shown here, still exists and is carefully preserved in the National Archives.

New York and Pennsylvania had chosen to oppose independence. South Carolina was undecided, and Maryland was wavering. Two days of debate showed no change in the positions of these colonies. Adams agreed to postpone a vote until July 1 to buy time.

A Declaration Is Prepared

On June 11, 1776, the Congress chose a committee to draft a document explaining why the Americans wanted independence, in case that was the final decision. On that committee were delegates John Adams, Benjamin Franklin, Thomas Jefferson, Robert Livingston, and Roger Sherman.

On June 28, the committee presented the proposed Declaration of Independence to the Congress. The

Securing Rights

"We hold these truths to be self-evident, that all men are created equal, that they are endowed by their creator with certain unalienable rights, that among these are life, liberty, and the pursuit of happiness. That to secure these rights, governments are instituted among men, deriving their just power from the consent of the governed. That whenever any form of government becomes destructive of these ends, it is the right of the people to alter or to abolish it, and to institute new government . . . as to them shall seem most likely to effect their safety and happiness."

Declaration of Independence, 1776

Independence Day

John Adams had predicted that future Americans would celebrate their independence on July 2, the day independence was decided. But it was July 4 —the day the Congress approved the Declaration of Independence—that became the nation's birthday. It is the Declaration, after all, that sets forth the basic principles on which the nation was founded and which it still follows today.

Adams probably worked harder than anyone else to persuade delegates to vote for independence. And Thomas Jefferson, with his stirring words, gave voice and meaning to the historic choice facing the Congress. It is an interesting coincidence that the two men, both of whom survived to a great age, died on Independence Day, 1826— the fiftieth anniversary of the Declaration's approval.

debate about independence began the following Monday, July 1. When John Adams counted votes, he found nine colonies in favor of independence. Delegates from New York—waiting for instructions from their assembly— would not commit, but Maryland had voted in favor. South Carolina still resisted, as did Pennsylvania. Delaware was tied.

Getting the Last Votes

Richard Henry Lee got South Carolina to agree that it would vote for the Lee Resolution if Delaware

This print from the 1700s shows a famous incident in New York City, when former colonists pulled down a statue of King George after independence was declared. The illustration was probably done from imagination as it shows slaves dressed in unlikely clothing doing the work.

and Pennsylvania did so. John Adams broke the Delaware deadlock by sending a messenger to summon pro-independence delegate Cesar Rodney, who was home with his sick wife. In Pennsylvania, meanwhile, three delegates favored independence and four, including John Dickinson, opposed it. But Adams convinced Dickinson and another delegate not to take their seats the next day, thereby switching the Pennsylvania vote to three-to-two in favor of the Lee Resolution. If Rodney voted, then independence would be approved.

On July 2, all proceeded as planned. Rodney, exhausted after racing 90 miles (145 km) from his home, arrived to break Delaware's tie. Eleven other colonies also voted for independence, and New York simply abstained. The delegates had decided on independence from Britain. Two days later—on July 4, 1776—the Congress approved the Declaration of Independence.

Americans Respond

The news of independence was met with joy around the country. The first public reading of the Declaration, in Philadelphia, took place on July 8, 1776. The crowd cheered, and the city's church bells rang in celebration. On July 10, a public reading in New York City inspired a crowd to pull down a statue of King George III. Later, the statue was melted down so the lead it was made from could be turned into musket balls. In Savannah, Georgia, a crowd burned the king in **effigy**. In Boston, Patriots tore the royal coats of arms off the State House.

Loyalists—of whom there were still plenty—held their tongues. They knew that, with all the celebrations going on, now was not the time to stand up for Britain. All they could do was hope that the British army and navy could suppress the rebellion before it got too far out of hand.

Signing the Declaration

On July 4, 1776, when the Declaration of Independence was approved, only two men signed it. They were the Congress's president, John Hancock, and secretary, Charles Thomson. The paper was then whisked off to a printer for copies to be made. About two weeks after the Declaration was approved, on July 19, the Congress ordered an official copy. That day, the Congress heard that the New York assembly had also approved independence. As a result, the printer was told to title the document a "unanimous declaration." On August 2, the delegates signed this final copy. Ironically, some who had actually voted for independence were no longer members of the Congress and did not sign it; some who signed it had not actually been in the Congress back on July 2. And some who had voted against independence decided to add their signatures.

Members of the Congress knew that by adding their names to the document they were committing treason against Britain. As a result, they withheld their names from the public until January 1777, when the war turned in their favor. The British still destroyed the homes of fifteen signers during the course of the American Revolution.

Time Line

1773 Boston Tea Party.

1774 September 1: Gage's troops seize Massachusetts' powder supplies.
September 5: First Continental Congress opens in Philadelphia.

1775 February 27: British fail in attempt to seize cannons in Salem.
April 19: Battle of Lexington and Concord.
May 10: Colonists capture Fort Ticonderoga in New York; Second Continental Congress opens in Philadelphia.
June 14: Congress makes plans to form American Continental Army.
June 17: Battle of Bunker Hill.
July 3: Washington takes official command of Patriot forces.
July 5: Congress approves Olive Branch Petition.
July 6: Congress approves "Declaration of the Causes and Necessities of Taking Up Arms."
July 26: Congress establishes post office for the colonies.
July 31: Congress rejects British plan of reconciliation.
August 23: George III declares colonies in open rebellion.
October: Congress votes to form American Continental Navy.
November 13: Patriot forces capture Montreal, Canada.
December: Patriot forces occupy Norfolk, Virginia.
December 31: Patriots attack Quebec, Canada.

1776 January 9: Thomas Paine's *Common Sense* is published.
February 27: Patriots defeat Loyalists at Moore's Creek Bridge, North Carolina.
March 4–5: American forces occupy Dorchester Heights south of Boston.
March 17–26: British evacuate Boston.
April 12: North Carolina becomes first colony to instruct delegates to Congress to vote for independence.
May 2: British forces in Quebec force Patriot army to retreat.
May 4: Rhode Island becomes first colony to declare independence from Britain.
June 7: Richard Henry Lee proposes Lee Resolution in favor of independence.
July 2: Congress votes in favor of independence.
July 4: Congress approves Declaration of Independence.

1781 Britain surrenders to Patriot forces at Yorktown, Virginia.

1783 Britain recognizes U.S. independence.

Glossary

arsenal: store of weapons and ammunition.

artillery: large heavy guns, such as cannons.

battery: artillery unit of several guns.

bayonet: blade attached to front end of a shoulder gun and used to stab the enemy in combat.

casualty: soldier or other person who is wounded, killed, or missing in battle.

colony: settlement, area, or country owned or controlled by another nation.

congress: meeting. The name "Congress" was given to the first meetings of delegates from the British colonies and was then adopted as the name of the U.S. legislature when the United States formed a national government.

constitution: document that lays down the basic rules and laws of a nation or organization.

delegate: person chosen to represent a group at a meeting or in making decisions.

diplomat: person who represents his or her country in a foreign country.

effigy: image or figure representing a person who is disliked.

frontier: edge of something known or settled. In the early years of the United States, the frontier meant the most westward point of white settlement.

garrison: military post; or the troops stationed at a military post.

legislature: group of officials that makes laws.

Loyalist: American who rejected independence and wanted the colonies to remain British.

mercenary: soldier who serves just for money, especially one hired by a foreign country to fight on its behalf.

militia: group of citizens organized into an army (as opposed to an army of professional soldiers, or regulars).

Patriot: American who supported the American Revolution; more generally, a person who is loyal to and proud of his or her country.

peninsula: piece of land jutting out into water but connected to mainland on one side.

redoubt: small fortification, usually built of earth or wood, where artillery was placed to fire at an enemy.

regular: professional soldier; member of a national army.

republic: nation that is led by elected officials and that has no monarch.

resolution: statement of principle by a legislative assembly.

siege: military operation in which a group of attackers surrounds a target and either attacks it or keeps it trapped in an attempt to force it to surrender.

Further Resources

Books

Ford, Barbara. *Paul Revere: Rider for the Revolution* (Historical American Biographies). Enslow, 1997.

Hakim, Joy. *From Colonies to Country* (A History of US volume 3). Oxford University Press, 2002.

Marcovitz, Hal. *The Declaration of Independence* (American Symbols and Their Meanings). Mason Crest, 2002.

Stratemeyer, Edward. *The Minute Boys of Lexington*. Lost Classics, 2001.

Uschan, Michael V. *Lexington and Concord* (Landmark Events in American History). World Almanac Library, 2004.

Places to Visit

Independence National Historic Park
143 South Third Street
Philadelphia, PA 19106
Telephone: (215) 965–2305

Web Sites

The History Place–American Revolution
www.historyplace.com/unitedstates/revolution
Historical web site offers information and images to do with the American Revolution.

Independence National Historic Park
www.nps.gov/inde/home.htm
National Park Service site has information about the Declaration of Independence and about historic sites such as Independence Hall and the home of the Liberty Bell.

Journals of the Continental Congress
memory.loc.gov/ammem/amlaw/lwjc.html
Records of the daily proceedings of the First and Second Continental Congresses as published by the Library of Congress.

LIBERTY! - The American Revolution
www.pbs.org/ktca/liberty/
Web site deriving from a six-part PBS television series about the American Revolution.

Index